FATHER HERMAN
ALASKA'S SAINT

FATHER HERMAN
Alaska's Saint

By F. A. Golder

Papercut illustrations by
Nikki McClure

St. HERMAN brd.

ST. HERMAN OF ALASKA BROTHERHOOD
2004

Address all correspondence to:
St. Herman of Alaska Brotherhood
P.O. Box 70
Platina, California 96076

sainthermanpress.com

Front cover: Papercut illustration by Nikki McClure.

First Edition, 1968
Second Edition, 1984
Third Edition, 2004

Publishers Cataloging-in-Publication

F. A. Golder, 1877–1929.
    Father Herman: Alaska's saint.

Library of Congress Control Number: 2003110571
ISBN: 1–887904–03–4

CONTENTS

St. Herman traveling near the shore of Spruce Island in an Alutiiq bairdarka.

Preface

This book begins with the first English-language account of the life of St. Herman of Alaska (1757–1836). The author of this Life, Frank Alfred Golder (1877–1929), was a Russian-born professor of history at Washington State College at Pullman. When the Life was originally published in the first part of the twentieth century, Fr. Herman was little known outside of Alaska and his Valaam Monastery in northern Russia. Many years later, in 1970, Fr. Herman was canonized by the Orthodox Church, and today he is revered worldwide, especially in the countries of America, Russia, Greece, Romania and Serbia.

The life of St. Herman presents not only a history of America's first saint but also the most important chapter in the chronicle of one native Alaskan tribe: the Alutiiq people of Kodiak Island and its vicinity.*

In 1741 Vitus Bering's expedition to the Gulf of Alaska opened up the region to an army of Russian traders and trappers, lured there by the plentiful supply of seal and sea otter pelts. By the end of the eighteenth century, Alaska had become a Russian territory, with outposts stretching across the Aleutian Isles to Sitka. Many of the Russians lived on equal terms with

---

* The language and culture of the Alutiiq people are distinct from those of the native peoples of the Aleutian Islands, who are known as Aleuts. Despite the differences in language and culture, the Alutiiqs and Aleuts share some similar traditions and customs.

the native peoples, dwelling in their traditional sod houses and adopting the local customs.* Some of the wealthier traders would even adopt young natives and send them back to Russia to be educated.

This, unfortunately, was not the rule everywhere. The fierce competition for the lucrative fur trade led to the sometimes brutal exploitation of the Alaskan natives. Specifically on Kodiak Island, Grigory Shelikov's and Ivan Golikov's trading company** was infamous for its abuse of the native peoples. The Kodiak men were enslaved in the hunting of sea otters, while the women were routinely abducted; hunger and physical abuse became common.

Into this grim situation St. Herman and the nine other Russian missionaries sailed in 1794. Despite the terrible conditions they endured—lack of food, insufficient clothing and shelter, and persecution by the Russian traders—the missionaries eagerly began their preaching of the Gospel. One would expect few of the natives to embrace the religion of a people they were resisting. Amazingly, the opposite occurred: almost every member of the Alutiiq tribe became Orthodox.

According to the records of the missionaries and the oral traditions of the native Alaskans themselves,*** a complete and voluntary conversion took place, one that had its origin as an

---

* "They [the Russians] appear to be perfectly content to live after the manner of native Indians of the country; partaking with equal relish and appetite their … food, adopting the same fashion, and using the same materials for their apparel." (G. Vancouver, *A Voyage of Discovery to the North Pacific Ocean and Round the World, 1791–1794,* vol. 4, ed. W. Lamb, London: Halluyt Society, 1984.)

** In 1799 the Shelikov-Golikov Company merged with another company to become the Russian-American Company.

*** See references to the testimony of the Alutiiq elder, Simeon (Sven Sr.) Haakanson in S. A. Mousalimas, *The Transition from Shamanism to Russian Orthodoxy in Alaska* (Oxford: Berghahn Books, 1994), pp. 55–63.

indigenous movement. Their simple religion had prepared them for the Gospel message, and when they heard it they found therein the fulfillment of their customs and traditions.

Although many of their beliefs were vague, they had a clear concept of a creator of the world, a creation narrative that paralleled the revelation of Genesis, and a recollection of a paradise that had been lost.*

St. Innocent of Alaska, a missionary of the mid-nineteenth century, conjectured that the Alaskans so readily accepted Christianity because of their many noble qualities. Chastity, patience, silence, and respect for parents and elders, were all considered important virtues. Above all these virtues, charity was held in the highest esteem. The native peoples would give their last piece of food to someone who was hungry. As Stephen Cherepanov, a leader among Russian hunters, recalled about the Alaskan natives: "We did not observe among them any special faith, except what is proper to any kind of faith. They live and act in everything very simply."**

Despite the foreshadowing of Christianity present in the indigenous religions, there were also many differences. The enslavement, branding and mutilation of prisoners were common; slaves were often killed upon their masters' death to serve them in the afterlife; polygamous marriages were the norm; forgiveness for breaking tribal rules was practically unknown; and, most importantly, a shamanistic philosophy overshadowed the entire culture.

The life of the Kodiak natives was one of fear and bondage to shamans and spirits that could restore or take life. It was not that all shamans purposefully worked evil, but evil worked

---

* Fr. Ivan [St. Innocent] Veniaminov, *Notes on the Islands of the Unalashka District*, trans. Lydia T. Black and R. H. Geoghegan, ed. Richard A. Pierce (Kingston, Ontario: The Limestone Press, 1984), pp. 217–22.

** Mousalimas, *Transition from Shamanism to Russian Orthodoxy*, p. 40.

through them because of their inability to control these spirits or their own emotions.* The natives viewed the world as being full of spirits, some appearing to be good, others obviously evil, but all needing appeasement. The shamans, donning masks representing these entities and performing ritual dances and chants, would fall into trances as they communed with these spirits. Often they would prophesy, heal, or seek revenge through the power of the spirits.

Strangely enough, it was these very shamans who prophesied the coming of the missionaries and the need to embrace their teaching. This took place not only in Kodiak but all over Alaska. As St. Innocent recorded: "Old Aleutian people assert that some of their famous shamans had predicted, long before the coming of the Russians, that white men with different customs would come to them from beyond the sea and that subsequently all Aleutian people would become just like the newcomers and live according to their manner. With the appearance of the Russians, they began to prophesy that in the east, over their islands, they saw a brilliant dawn or a great light, and in it many people resembling the newcomers, while in the lower world, of the people whom they had seen there before, very few remained and it had become impenetrably dark there."**

With the arrival of St. Herman and the rest of the mission in Kodiak, the Alutiiqs were presented with paragons of the Christian life. Here were men who had given their whole lives to God, sacrificing everything to bring the Gospel to the natives of Alaska. The grace of the Holy Spirit worked in them and through them. The missionaries healed, fed, and taught the natives, working greater miracles than the shamans, and bringing light with no darkness. They are most remembered for their defense of the natives against the excesses of the Russian traders.

* Ibid., p. 178
** Veniaminov, *Notes*, p. 219.

Despite receiving death threats, the monks reprimanded Russian-American Company officials and reported back to the Tsarist Government the dismal treatment of the natives who were now legally protected as Russian subjects.* Finally, the missionaries "sought, as best can be determined from the archives, to present Christianity as the fulfillment of what Alaskans already knew rather than its replacement."**

Due to all these factors, nearly the entire Kodiak native population was baptized within a year of the Russian missionaries' arrival. The letters of the missionaries and the oral traditions of the Alutiiqs tell us that the newly enlightened people brought forth their shamanist tools and destroyed them of their own accord.

This, however, did not signal the destruction of the native culture. Already in the early 1800s, the Alutiiq language was being taught in Kodiak schools, and many natives were bi-lingual (Russian and Alutiiq). Throughout Alaska church services were translated into native dialects. In 1829 the Gospel according to St. Matthew appeared in the Unangan Aleut language and in 1848 in Alutiiq. Far from eradicating native languages, the missionaries created the first alphabets, primers and translations of basic explanations of Christianity. The acquisition of their own written language gave the Alaskans an increased sense of nationhood and the ability to further define their culture. As early as 1870 one visitor to Kodiak noted that "Most of the people can read."***

---

* Despite protests from the Russian-American Company officials, the missionaries had the Alutiiqs swear the Russian Oath of Allegiance, which automatically gave them protection as Russian subjects.

** Michael Oleksa, ed., *Alaskan Missionary Spirituality* (Mahwah, New Jersey: Paulist Press, 1987), p. 13.

*** Eli Huggins, *Kodiak and Afognak Life, 1868-1870* (Ontario: Limestone Press, 1981), p. 13.

It is a fact that during the transition from shamanism to Christianity many traditions were abandoned. In general, however, this was a voluntary discarding of customs that were incompatible with Christianity (e.g., the killing of slaves). Traditional songs and dances continued to be performed, but shamanistic rituals were abandoned. Talents and energy that had been poured into carving spirit masks were now enlisted in the painting of icons and the carving of church adornments.*

The Alaskans themselves took key roles in a Church which had become their own. In 1826 the first priest of native ancestry was ordained. He went on to become a great missionary, translator and pastor: St. Yakov Netsvetov. Native priests, deacons, readers, and church wardens soon became a common sight. Today a seminary in Kodiak continues to prepare native Alaskans for the priesthood. Over the two-hundred-year period since the arrival of the Russian mission, the peoples of Alaska have produced saints, martyrs, and numerous righteous ones.**

The second half of the nineteenth century brought new challenges to the Church in Alaska. In 1867 the United States purchased Alaska from Russia. Although the treaty guaranteed the rights of natives to remain Orthodox Christians, these articles were largely ignored by U.S. officials and Protestant missionaries. At the end of the nineteenth century many Alaskans could speak Russian, English and a native language, but were still considered uncivilized by the authorities. A systematic persecution of the native and Orthodox culture was initiated. Russian and native languages were forbidden to be used in

* Michael Oleksa, *Orthodox Alaska, a Theology of Mission* (Crestwood, N.Y.: St. Vladimir's Seminary Press), p. 154.

** Of particular interest is the story of John Smirennikov. See Paul D. Garret, *St. Innocent, Apostle to America* (Crestwood, N.Y.: St. Vladimir's Seminary Press), pp. 77–85.

schools. Soon a policy of assimilation was implemented, and the traditional life of the Alaskans began to wane.*

Despite the loss of traditional culture in the twentieth century, most Kodiak natives still consider the Orthodox Church to be their own. Today, in spite of the challenges faced by the natives and the Church, the ordination of Alaskan priests and the preservation of native language and culture by village elders gives hope that a great harvest for Christ will continue to spring from the island of Kodiak.

This book presents the life and miracles of the first sower of this good soil, St. Herman. His life brought forth great fruit, a new Christian nation. Out of darkness, bondage, and fear, the Alutiiq Nation turned to the light of Christ, finding every good thing they had possessed multiplied a thousandfold in the Orthodox Church.

The author of the brief Life that follows, F. A. Golder, devoted his life to the study of the Northwest of this continent, and became a leading authority on it. While doing research work in Russia in 1914 he visited Valaam Monastery, where he put down in his notes the monastery version of St. Herman's Life and published it some years later in booklet form in Pullman, Washington, using it as a little Christmas gift to send to his friends. It was written with evident sympathy towards the Saint. Thus, the first Life of Fr. Herman in English, written over fifty years before his canonization, already calls him "Alaska's Saint."

—Ryassaphore-monk Adrian
St. Herman of Alaska Monastery
Platina, California

---

* For a detailed account of the suppression of Alaskan culture and Orthodoxy, see Oleksa, *Orthodox Alaska, a Theology of Mission*, pp. 171–86, and Sergei Kan, *Memory Eternal: Tlingit Culture and Russian Orthodox Christianity Through Two Centuries* (Seattle: University of Washington Press, 1999).

St. Herman arriving at Valaam Monastery.

PART I

THE LIFE OF FR. HERMAN

By F. A. Golder

An Introductory Note
by the Author

Dᴜʀɪɴɢ July 1914, I spent two delightful weeks in Valaam Monastery, situated on the beautiful Valaam Island in Lake Ladoga. While there the friendly monks told me of Fr. Herman and guided me to the printed and manuscript materials on the subject which I have here made use of in writing this little book. This is not a critical study of the life of Fr. Herman but the monastery version. In this respect it does not differ from the lives of other saints. It is a pleasure to be able to testify publicly to the simple but whole-hearted hospitality of the monastery, the saintliness of the abbot, the kindliness of the brothers, the beauty of the religious service and the sweetness of the music. I appreciate deeply all their favors, especially the standing invitation to become one of their number.

—F. A. Golder

Eᴅɪᴛᴏʀs' Nᴏᴛᴇ: In the Life of St. Herman that follows, the editors have made some slight alterations for the sake of accuracy. The footnotes have been supplied by the editors.

I

A Valaam Monk

THE Alaskan traveler who visits Kodiak in the summer
never forgets the beauty of the island, the arcadian village
of St. Paul, the blue sea, the green hills, the grassy slopes, the
flowery valleys, the babbling brooks, the plaintive note of the
golden crowned sparrow. Kodiak is well worth remembering
for other reasons: it is of historic importance, it is a sacred spot.
The first Christian missionaries in the American Northwest
landed on this island and the first Christian church in our
North Pacific was built in this village. There is still another
reason: for over forty years a man of God, Fr. Herman, lived
and labored among the people of Kodiak and the neighboring
islands. They still revere his memory, treasure his sayings, glory
in his deeds, and adore him as a saint. It is the purpose of this
little book to tell the story of this holy man as it is told by the
natives of Kodiak and by his brother monks.

Fr. Herman was born not far from Moscow about the year
1757; but neither the exact place of his birth nor his name before becoming a monk is known. It would seem that his parents were of the merchant class and they gave him some
educational advantages, enough to read the New Testament
and the *Lives of the Saints.* At the age of sixteen he entered the
Holy Trinity-St. Sergius Monastery, but did not live in the

St. Herman fishing at Valaam Monastery.

monastery proper but in one of its isolated stations near the Gulf of Finland, where he was undisturbed in his devotions. While in this place he had reason to believe that the Holy Virgin had taken him under her special care. A sore broke out under his chin, causing him much suffering and slowly undermining his strength. In his sorrow he spent the whole night praying and weeping before the image of Our Lady. Towards the morning he wiped the picture with a cloth, which he then wrapped over the sore, and fell on the floor exhausted. In his sleep he saw the Virgin standing near him and felt her touching his swollen face. He woke with a start and found himself well; the sore was gone and only a slight scar was left to remind him of the miraculous cure.

In this deserted spot he lived five or six years and then entered the Valaam Monastery, situated on Valaam Island in Lake Ladoga. Fr. Herman was attracted by the solitude of Valaam, which during six months of the year is ice-bound and during the other six months is reached only with difficulty. The monastery was far removed from the temptations of the world and was famed for its piety. Fr. Herman's attractive personality and kindly ways soon made him a favorite with the other monks, so much so that even to this day they speak of him as the holiest man that has ever gone from them. They point to the place named after him, *Germanova,* where he was wont to wander off and pray for days at a time until the brothers had to go and bring him back. They tell of his religious ardor, of his gentleness, and of his sweet tenor voice, which was like that of an angel. Fr. Herman had the soul of a poet and there was much about the monastery and the island that appealed to his sense of beauty: the flowery fields, the shady forests, the wild birds, the snow-clad trees, the ice-covered lake, the mighty wind and raging storm. It was one of his duties to catch the fish with which to feed the hungry multitudes who came to pray. On such occasions Fr. Herman would pull away from shore and, after casting his nets, sit and contemplate in secret silence his beloved Valaam, its white walls and green woods, golden domes and blue sky, picturesque chapels and emerald isles, holy shrines and towering cliffs. From afar he watched the procession of the pilgrim bands with banners flying and candles glimmering and listened to the sweet music and the chiming of the bells as they came floating through the balmy air and over the silvery sea. To the fisherman Valaam was Jerusalem the Golden.

> *Oh, sweet and blessed country,*
> *The home of God's elect.*

But more than his surroundings he loved his fellow monks, their simplicity, their humility, their guilelessness, their child-likeness. Their time was not spent in scholastic disputations and literary compositions, but in toiling in the fields and working in the shops, in feeding the hungry and praying with the dying. Years afterwards, when enduring the curses of Baranov and the sneers of his minions, Fr. Herman's mind fondly turned to the days of his young manhood, to his Valaam, to his brothers. In a letter written to the abbot in 1795, he says: "The frightful places of Siberia cannot destroy, the black forests cannot hide, the mighty rivers cannot efface, the stormy ocean cannot put out the warm affection that I have for my beloved Valaam. Often I close my eyes, and see you across the waters."

2

The American Mission

W HEN IN 1793 the Holy Synod decided to organize a Kodiak Mission and called for volunteers to go to America to preach the Gospel to the Alaskan natives, Fr. Herman was one of the first to offer himself and one of the first to be accepted. This was no ordinary undertaking; it was the first mission ever sent out by Russia across the sea. The men selected were the best the monastery had to offer, they were full of the spirit of the Apostles, and they were eager to give their lives to advance the Kingdom of God. They were ten in number: Archimandrite Ioasaph the leader, monks Juvenaly, Makary, Afanasy, Ioasaph, Herman, deacons Stephen and Nektary, and two acolytes, Dimitry and Nikita. These men were plain peasant and fisher folk of limited education and restricted outlook, but zealous in the faith and ardent in their devotions.* They had never been far from their village

---

* The information here is not entirely precise. Hierodeacon Stephen, former officer, and Hieromonk Juvenaly, at one time a mining engineer, were not of such simple background as the author states. As for the Archimandrite Ioasaph (before monasticism Ivan Ilyich Bolotoff), the son of a priest, he was educated in Tver and Yaroslavl Seminaries. Later he taught for four years in the Uglich Theological School. In 1784 he entered the monastic life, and in 1793 he was appointed head of the Kodiak Mission.

homes and out-of-the-way monasteries, and the journey to the new field of labor was an important event in their lives. They set out from Moscow on January 22, 1794, and moved gradually across Siberia to Okhotsk, where they took ship for Kodiak, reaching their destination on September 24 of that same year.

As soon as they walked ashore the leader called his followers together on a knoll to discuss plans for the work. It is inspiring to read the account of this first religious conference in the Northwest and to note with what eagerness the brothers contended among themselves for the most difficult and dangerous task. It is said that one of the monks, while walking along the beach, saw an empty skiff into which he stepped and, lifting his hands to heaven, prayed that he might be guided to a place where he could be of most service. A wind came up and blew the skiff to Nuchek and there the monk preached salvation to the natives.

The winter that followed their arrival was a busy one for Fr. Herman and the other missionaries, who went from village to village telling the people of the Saviour. On May 19, 1795 the Archimandrite wrote: "The Lord be praised! We have baptized more than seven thousand Americans and have performed more than two thousand marriage ceremonies…. We love them and they love us; they are good but poor. They are so willing to be baptized that they have destroyed and burned their idolatrous things. We were afraid that they were naked, but God be thanked they are not altogether without modesty … their bird-skin shirts come down sufficiently far in front…." During the year 1795 Hieromonk Juvenaly baptized seven hundred natives on Nuchek and all the inhabitants of Cook Inlet. In the following summer he crossed over to the mainland and exhorted the people living along the shores of Iliamna Lake to give up their polygamous and heathenish practices and lead Christian lives. Many heeded his words and were baptized; but

The arrival of the Valaam missionaries on Kodiak Island.

others, led by their shamans, sought to destroy him. Paddling into the village of Quinhagak near the mouth of the Kuskokwim with his native guide, he was viciously attacked by hunters under the direction of a shaman. As Fr. Juvenaly stood blessing them, the hunters let loose their bowstrings, killing him in a hail of arrows.

The work so auspiciously begun aroused much interest in Russia. The Holy Synod decided to enlarge the field of labor and to increase the force of workers. It called Archimandrite Ioasaph to Irkutsk to be consecrated bishop so that on his return he would train and ordain native priests who should go over the length and breadth of the Northwest to carry light to those who lived in darkness. This grand conception, promising so much for the glory of God, was never realized. The ship Phoenix, the first boat built in Alaska, on which the bishop with his assistants, including Frs. Makary, Stephen, and others, was returning from Okhotsk to Kodiak in 1799, foundered at sea with all on board. From this sad loss the mission never fully recovered.*

There were still four missionaries in America and, under the guidance of Fr. Herman, they could have continued the work had they not been so bitterly opposed by the officers of the Russian American Company. It was the old fight between the missionary and the trader. The priests reproached Baranov and his associates for their licentious lives and for their brutal treatment of the islanders, and later brought the matter before the Holy Synod. Baranov neither forgot nor forgave this injury and he swore that he would be avenged on the informers. As soon as it became known that the bishop was lost, Baranov set about venting his wrath on Fr. Herman and his fellow workers. He was all-powerful, he was coarse, he was cruel. It used to be a common saying among the hunters of his day, that, "God is in

* *Outline of the History of the American Orthodox Mission* (in Russian) (St. Petersburg: Valaam Monastery, 1894).

Heaven, the Tsar is in Russia, Baranov is in America; let us, therefore, bow before Baranov." He drove the monks from the natives and unmercifully abused the natives if they went near the monks. By dragging one of their number to the church and threatening to hang him from the steeple, Baranov secured the keys to the building and kept it locked after that. He was determined to hound the missionaries from the island and out of his sight; and at the same time his friends in the capital were powerful enough to oppose the petitions of the poor men to be allowed to return to Russia. They were caught between the devil Baranov and the deep Pacific Ocean. These adversities and discouragements crushed the independent spirit of Fr. Herman's associates; they lost confidence in themselves and the respect of the people. After much pleading Fr. Nektary was allowed, in 1806, to go to Siberia; Fr. Afanasy, weak in body and spirit, retired to Afognak; Fr. Ioasaph became demoralized and dragged out a pitiful existence in the village of St. Paul. Fr. Herman alone remained steadfast in the Faith. Trials and tribulations made him only stronger, and he would under no circumstances desert his people and let them slip back into the power of the devil. Realizing, however, that the cause of God could be advanced more quickly away from Baranov and his satanic crew, Fr. Herman withdrew from their presence and opened a mission on the uninhabited island of Elovoi (Spruce), which he named New Valaam in memory of the Holy Island in Lake Ladoga.

3

Spruce Island

Nᴇᴡ Vᴀʟᴀᴀᴍ is a small island not many miles from Kodiak. Here the father built himself a cell, a chapel, and a house to accommodate the native orphan children. After a time a number of Alutiiq* families settled on the island, but they lived some distance from the father, who sought a life of solitude. A man asked him once: "Fr. Herman, do you live alone in the forest? Do you never become lonely?" "No, I am not alone," he said, "God is there as He is everywhere. His angels are there. Is it possible to be lonely in their society? Is it not better to be in their company than in that of people?"

A traveler who saw Fr. Herman in 1819 described him as of medium height and delicate constitution. His face was pale and kindly and his soft blue eyes invited confidence and bespoke sympathy. His gentle and friendly voice drew people to him, especially the children. His body was girded with a fifteen-pound chain, his shirt was a deer hide, his sandals a piece of rough leather, though at times he went barefoot, and over all he wore a patched monastic cloak. Thus scantily clad

---

* Since this Life of St. Herman was written before the distinction was commonly made between Alutiiqs and Aleuts (see the note on p. 7 above), F. A. Golder refers to the Alutiiqs as Aleuts. We have changed his text to render the more precise term "Alutiiqs."

he walked over hill and dale, through snow and rain, in heat and in cold, wherever duty called him. A bench covered with a seal skin served for a bed, two bricks for a pillow, and a board for a blanket. His personal habits were simple: he ate sparingly, slept little, prayed long and worked hard. He was tolerant of the weaknesses of others and did not urge them to lead the same ascetic life he did. He was kind to wild animals, the birds and the squirrels were his companions, and the savage bear fed out of his hand.

If he led a secluded life it was not in order to escape the cares of the world, for whenever his presence could serve some useful purpose he came forth. His great object in life was to help and uplift the Alutiiqs, whom he regarded as mere children in need of protection and guidance. He was ever pleading for them with the officers of the company. "I, the lowest servant of these poor people," he wrote to Yanovsky, "with tears in my eyes ask this favor: be our father and protector. I have no fine speeches to make, but from the bottom of my heart I pray you to wipe the tears from the eyes of the defenseless orphans, relieve the suffering of the oppressed people and show them what it means to be merciful."

Fr. Herman was a nurse of the natives in a literal as well as a figurative sense. When an epidemic broke out in Kodiak and carried off scores of people, he never left the village, but went from house to house, nursing the sick, comforting the afflicted and praying with the dying. It is no wonder that the natives loved him and came from afar to hear him tell the story of Christ and His love for them. Fr. Herman fed the hungry, cheered the troubled, turned strife into concord, and all who came to him discouraged he sent away with God's peace in their hearts. He gave to the orphan children a home, he taught them to read and write, and trained them to do useful and honest work. His daily food he secured through his own efforts

St. Herman and the orphan children gardening on Spruce Island.

and with the help of his pupils. They planted gardens, caught fish, picked wild berries, and dried mushrooms. His influence over the people was remarkable. One Sunday morning he told the natives that Jesus gave His life to save humanity and that it was the duty of every person to help mankind. When he had concluded, a young woman, Sophia Vlasova, stepped up and offered herself for God's service. The good father saw the hand of God in this sacrifice, for at the time he was in need of a woman to look after his little children, and made Sophia the matron of the orphanage.

The Alutiiqs were not the only people for whom he labored. Fr. Herman worked with equal zeal in behalf of the white men and through his efforts many were led to give up their lives of sin and follow the teachings of the Saviour. One of his converts was Baranov's successor, Yanovsky, who when he reached Kodiak boasted of his free-thinking and spoke contemptuously of Christianity. He heard of the pious monk and invited him over to Kodiak where night after night the two men discussed questions of faith, immortality, and salvation. The simple words and strong faith of the monk sank deeply into the heart of the naval officer, and years later he and his son and daughters gave up all that they possessed and entered monasteries. Another of his converts was an educated German sea-captain in the employ of the company. He engaged the father in a religious argument and before it ended the captain acknowledged his errors, renounced the heretical doctrines of Luther, and asked to be received into the Orthodox Church.

One day the captain and officers of a Russian man-of-war invited Fr. Herman on board to dine with them. In the course of the conversation he put this question to them. "What do you, gentlemen, regard as most worthy of love and what do you most wish for your happiness?" One man said he desired riches, a second glory, a third a beautiful wife, a fourth the command of a fine ship. The others present expressed themselves in some similar manner. "Is it not true," said Fr. Herman, "that all your wishes can be summarized in this short sentence: each of you desires that which he thinks is most worthy of love?" To this statement they all agreed. "If this is true," he continued, "what can there be better, higher, nobler, and more worthy of love than the Lord Jesus Christ, the Creator of heaven and earth, the Author of all living beings, Who provides for all, Who loves all, and Who is the incarnation of love? Should we not above all love God, seek Him and desire Him?" The officers were quite confused and replied that what he said was true, was self-evident. He then asked them if they loved God. "To be sure," said they, "we love God. How could anyone not love Him?" Hearing these words the old man bowed his head and said: "I, a poor sinner, for forty years have tried to love God and I cannot say that I love Him as I should. To love God is to think of Him always, to serve Him day and night, and to do His will. Do you, gentlemen, love God in this manner, do you often pray to Him, do you always do His will?" With shame they acknowledged their shortcomings. "Then let me beseech you, my friends, that from this day forth, from this hour, from this minute, you will love God above all." The officers marveled at his words and long remembered them.

Whenever the workmen of the company got into difficulty with their officers, they besought Fr. Herman to intercede for them. Though old, feeble and blind, he was always ready to undertake these offices of mercy. One day he pleaded hard with the agent in Kodiak in behalf of a hunter, trying to point out to the officer the Christian duty of forgiveness and the need of charity; but it was to no purpose. The hardheartedness of the man moved the old father to tears and he exclaimed: "Woe unto him who is not merciful, for no mercy shall be shown to him!" The wife of the agent, who was standing by, retorted by saying: "Fr. Herman, we are merciful and we give charity four times a year." "What you give to the poor belongs to God and not to you. There will come a time when you, too, will be in trouble and in want and then you will know what mercy means." Turning to the agent he added: "In two years from now you will be transferred to a less desirable place and you will then think of my words." As he said so it came to pass: two years later the agent was carried in chains to Sitka.

Because he was so outspoken in his condemnation of all that was coarse and wicked, there were some who hated him and sought to do him harm. One night a party of the company's men invaded his cell in search of furs and money which, they claimed, he had taken from the Alutiiqs. They ransacked his hut from top to bottom without finding anything of value. This angered them and one of the men took up an axe and commenced tearing up the floor in the hopes of discovering something incriminating. Fr. Herman watched them sorrowfully and said: "My friend, you have lifted up the axe to no good purpose, for by it you shall die." Not many months afterwards this man with others was sent to Cook Inlet to put down a native uprising, and one night a hostile native stole into the camp, picked up the axe and slew him with it.

In 1834 Baron Ferdinand Wrangell, at the time a captain in the Imperial Navy, arrived in Kodiak and went unannounced to make a call on the old father, who was then seventy-eight years of age and blind. Notwithstanding that, he knew who his visitor was and greeted him with the title of "Admiral." Captain Wrangell tried to set him right but the old man told him that on such and such a day he had been named "Admiral," which, as it later proved, was really true.

4

Alaska's Saint

WHEN Fr. Herman first came to New Valaam, the devil and his agents tried to get him into their power. They presented themselves to him in the form of human beings to tempt him and in the shape of wild beasts to frighten him; but they wrought no evil in him, for by calling on the Saints he drove them off. He was ever on guard against their machinations, and he permitted no one to engage him in conversation or to enter his cell without first making the Sign of the Cross.

As he grew older and holier the good father was allowed to see angels, he was given control over the elements, and was granted the gift of prophecy. On certain holy nights* he watched by the seaside for the angels to appear and dip the cross in the water, and this holy water he gave to the sick and cripples and they became whole. When an inundation threatened to submerge New Valaam, Fr. Herman checked its force by placing the icon of the Holy Virgin on the beach and ordering the tidal wave not to advance beyond it. Another time he saved his people from a forest fire by marking the limits

---

* On the feast of the Baptism of our Lord the Holy Church blesses water to be used by the faithful throughout the whole year. After 1825 there was no priest in the Kodiak area to perform this blessing. His disciple Gerasim reported having seen an angel bless the waters of the bay for Fr. Herman.

beyond which the flames were not to spread. A year before it was generally known in Kodiak, he told the Alutiiqs that the Metropolitan of Moscow had passed away. He foretold that an epidemic was coming which would kill off a large part of the native population and that those who were left living would be gathered into fewer villages. Two or three years before his death he told an agent of the company that the time was not far off when a bishop would be appointed for Alaska. The prophecies just mentioned have already come to pass, and other prophecies made by him will come true in God's good time.

When Fr. Herman realized that his days on earth were numbered and that it was time to join the saints, he called to him Sophia Vlasova with the girls and Gerasim, his helper. He asked that Sophia spend the remainder of her years on the island and that when she died she be buried at his feet. He advised the girls to marry and the same advice he gave to Gerasim, whom he asked to make his home on New Valaam. Continuing, he said: "When I die, don't send for a priest; he will never come! Do not wash my body. Put it on a board, fold my hands on my chest, place me in my monk's mantle; with its lappets cover my face, and with the klobuk my head. If anyone wishes to bid farewell to me, let him kiss my cross. Do not show my face to anybody."* Several days after the above conversation he called for Gerasim to light the candles and read from the Acts of the Apostles. While Gerasim was reading the countenance of the old father was lighted up with a heavenly light and he was heard to say, "Glory to Thee, O Lord." He then told Gerasim to put aside the holy book, for God had granted him another week of life. At the end of that time he again summoned Gerasim and requested him to light the candles and to read from the Acts of the Apostles. In the midst of the reading Gerasim became aware that the cell was filled with

* The face is to be covered according to the monastic practice.

The repose of St. Herman.

light and that a halo played around the holy father's head. Gerasim then knew that Father Herman was a saint and that he had gone to join the heavenly choir.*

On the night that Fr. Herman died the people of Afognak Island saw hovering over New Valaam a column of light. At this wonderful sight they fell on their knees exclaiming, "Our holy man has gone from us." In another village the people observed that same night an object like a human being borne aloft from New Valaam towards Heaven.

Gerasim and the girls became frightened at what they had witnessed and immediately dispatched a messenger to Kodiak to tell what had happened. The officer of the company sent back word not to inter the body until he came over with a priest and a casket. But before he could start, there blew up such a storm as had never been seen, and no one dared to venture out to sea for a whole month. During that whole time the body of the Saint lay in his cell without any decomposition setting in. Seeing the hand of God in the storm and recalling Fr. Herman's last words, Gerasim and the girls buried the father according to his wishes. Immediately the wind died down, the sea became calm, and the sun came out.

In 1842 the ship on which Bishop Innocent was sailing from Kamchatka to Alaska ran into a severe storm which threatened to wreck it. The good bishop prayed for help to the saints, and remembering the pious Fr. Herman he said to himself, "If you have pleased God, Fr. Herman, make the wind change." Immediately a fair wind sprung up and in good time the boat was safe in the harbor of St. Paul. In gratitude for the deliverance, the bishop held a service over the grave of Fr. Herman.

* According to the research of Michael Z. Vinokouroff, an archivist of the Library of Congress, St. Herman reposed on November 15/28, 1836. See "Finding the True Date of St. Herman's Repose," *The Orthodox Word,* no. 131 (1986), pp. 283–85, 294.

Thirty years after the death of the Saint the priest of Kodiak visited his resting place and found that the grass on the grave is ever green, summer and winter, and that the cross is as new and as sound as the day it went up.

The natives of Kodiak love to tell the story of Fr. Herman, Alaska's Saint, who is so near and dear to them. He left no picturesque missions or learned colleges to speak of his achievements, but he planted Christianity in the hearts of the Alutiiqs and that shall endure as long as the Alutiiqs live. On the walls of Valaam Monastery may be seen hanging a picture of New Valaam and a likeness of Fr. Herman, and as the monks pass by they cross themselves and pray that the time may soon come when his bones shall rest in the sacred ground of the monastery and when the Church shall officially recognize him as a saint.*

* On July 27/August 9, 1970, St. Herman was simultaneously canonized by the Orthodox Church in America and the Russian Orthodox Church Outside of Russia.

St. Herman subduing a tidal wave by his prayers (see p. 33).

PART II

MIRACLES OF FR. HERMAN

Introduction to the Miracles

Throughout his life and up to the present day, St. Herman has interceded for those in need. The astonishing miracles of the subduing of a tidal wave and a forest fire are well known to any reader of the Saint's Life. Less well known are the numerous miracles that affected the daily lives of those around him. Many of these accounts have been passed down to our own time through the oral traditions of the Alutiiq people: angelic singing filled the Saint's forest, he multiplied fish for the hungry, and he foresaw the future of those around him.

After the Saint's repose, those who had known him as a miracle worker continued to ask for his assistance. The sick and suffering would turn to their beloved protector, and their pleas would not fall on deaf ears. Even up until recent times, native hunters and fishers would come to the Saint's grave asking his blessing before embarking on their work. Now a new generation of believers comes to the Saint's grave asking peace and healing for their souls and bodies.

We present here a selection of the miracles that have been gathered over the years. May they inspire others to call upon Apa* Herman, Alaska's and all America's protector.

_____

* "Apa" is the Alutiiq word for "father."

1. A RESCUE AT SEA
1842

In I. Barsukov's thorough biography of Metropolitan Innocent Veniaminov, the latter's daughter Catherine I. Petelin
describes the situation preceding the miracle of Fr. Herman's
intercession thus:

"For five days we were sailing to Spruce Island; the wind
was favorable. At night prior to the fifth day all of a sudden everybody on the ship felt a strong tremor and rocking, and all
were terrified. Bishop Innocent and the ship's captain came out
on the deck at eleven p.m. to find out what was the matter, but
there was nothing noticeable. The wind was blowing as before:
favorable and even. They asked the boatswain and the pilot
what it meant; they answered that a big change should be expected. Then the bishop and the captain understood that it
was an earthquake, although it did not last long, for a minute
or two only. And then, indeed, opposing winds began to blow,
strong and freezing; the sea began to spray foam and bluster;
the storm shook and tossed the vessel. One wave after another
furiously hurled themselves against the ship, gushing across the
deck. The passengers hid themselves in the hold and cabins.
The ship was not a large one, but it carried seventy passengers
aboard. All the hatches were hammered tight. Only the crew
remained above with their captain and the bishop. The rest of
the passengers remained without daylight in the hold, sitting
by candle-light. For twenty-eight days and nights the leaky
boat was drifting on the waves, rocking so hard that it was im-
possible to walk, so that the people were crowded together in a
sitting position for days on end, and everyone's legs were sore.
To endure twenty-eight days in a sitting position and in abso-
lute darkness, and at that almost without food and drink, was

extremely hard…. Also, there was not even dry bread; only some dust from it remained. Water also was scarce; only a half bottle of it was given out to four persons to last for twenty-four hours. At last there was no more water, and then we would squeeze water out of the sails and drink it. The salt meat was boiled in sea-water and distributed among passengers in small pieces. Everyone became ill…."*

Here is how the blessed Archbishop Innocent himself describes the event, in a letter to the Abbot of Valaam Monastery, Damascene, from Blagoveshchensk town, dated March 1, 1867:

"In 1842, while sailing to Kodiak, we were a long time** at sea and found ourselves in such desperate straits that we were left with less than half a barrel of water for fifty-two passengers. And in front of the entrance to Kodiak harbor we encountered an adverse wind that kept up constantly for three days and nights. Our boat went back and forth (or, in sailors' language, tacked) between the southern cape of Kodiak and Spruce Island, where Fr. Herman lived and died. Towards evening on the third day, when our boat was approaching Spruce Island again (for perhaps the twentieth or thirtieth time), I glanced at it and said mentally: 'If you, Fr. Herman, have pleased God, then let the wind change.' And indeed, it must have been no more than a quarter of an hour before the wind became suddenly favorable, and the very same evening we entered the bay and cast anchor. We did not serve a Moleben right then, however. A little later I went to the grave and served a Pannikhida for the dead—but without seeing any kind of vision.

"More than this I know nothing, and I have heard nothing similar from anyone concerning Fr. Herman.

---

* Ivan Barsukov, *Innocent, Metropolitan of Moscow and Kolomna* (Moscow, 1883), p. 171.

** Twenty-eight days, as another letter of Archbishop Innocent specifies.

"And so, committing myself to your prayers, I have the honor to be, with sincere brotherly love in the Lord,

"The well-wishing servant of Your Eminent Holiness,

"Innocent, Archbishop of Kamchatka."

2. HELP IN FINDING THINGS
1904

On Spruce Island, on the site of Starets* Herman's cell, there stood at the beginning of this century a small wooden memorial with an icon lamp that was always lit. It was maintained by an old man, Z. Ruppe, who kept watch, without pay, over the chapel at the grave of Fr. Herman. He looked after the chapel and showed it to pilgrims and visitors. On the eighth of August in the year 1904, a missionary-priest from the church in Kodiak, Fr. Tikhon Shalamov, visited Spruce Island, where Z. Ruppe personally told him about the supernatural help he had received from Fr. Herman himself.

Here is how he noted this in his travel-diary, *Along the Missions* (New York, 1904):

"Not long ago the old man Z. Ruppe was honored by seeing the Blessed Starets face to face. He had lost the key to the chapel and had searched for it for a long, long time without success in every nook and cranny of the house. Having given up all hope of finding it, he had already unscrewed the lock to the Church, so that he could open the church to pilgrims, when at night in a light sleep he saw the blessed Starets and heard a voice saying, 'Why are you searching so much? The key is in your satchel on the wall.' Ruppe got up immediately and found the key in the satchel."

—Priest Tikhon Shalamov

* *Starets*: the Russian word for "Elder."

3. HEALING FROM TUBERCULOSIS
1907

I was born in Kodiak and lived there when this miracle happened. When I was two or three years old I became very sick. Dr. Silverman was in charge of my case and from his medical point of view my trouble was tubercular hip. My leg would go up towards my back, causing terrible pain. What could they do at that date but to keep me in bed and as comfortable as possible? I was perfectly willing, as I was much too ill and in pain to do otherwise. They did try to stretch my leg by a can full of sand attached to my leg, and each day they added to the weight more sand. When I was able to walk I had to walk on crutches. By the time I was seven years old my sick leg was smaller than the other one and still causing pain.

On Spruce Island they had services once in a while. Some summer day in 1907 we went there on a hired little private passenger boat. On the way I got terrible pains which would not stop. When we arrived, they put tents on the beach to eat and sleep in. There were some thirty to forty people, including Fr. Kashevarov and the choir singers. At night I got worse and could not sleep the whole night.

In the morning everybody went to the church, which had been built over the grave of Fr. Herman. A tiny, narrow path leads to it through thick woods. It exhausted me. I had crutches and was crying from pain, hardly moving. Then Mother took me on her back, hoping to speed the distance, but it did not help since I was too heavy for her. And no one could help us because we were left far behind.

At the chapel they would not start the service because I needed confession and they waited and waited for us. Then five young men came and carried me on their arms like a baby, right to the church steps. I used crutches to come to the coffin with the remains of Fr. Herman, which is in the middle of the chapel, a little to the right. By the coffin I was about to lay my crutches on the floor, when they slipped under me and I fell with all my body on the coffin, head down, in full exhaustion. And I cried and prayed to Fr. Herman.

Then, all of a sudden, something happened to me! The pain was all gone. I felt I was not tired any more. I stood up and walked away from the coffin without crutches across the church to where Mother stood, to the great surprise of everyone. Since I was two years old I always used crutches to walk—this was the first time I walked without them as I walked to Mother. The whole church assembly gasped in amazement, being a witness to it. I stood next to Mother throughout the whole service and walked to receive Communion. After the service we went back to the tents on the beach to eat and I walked the self-same path as easily as if I was on air, without touching the ground. But Mother insisted that I use crutches, fearing I should fall. After dinner everyone went to pick berries, including myself, and we walked way past the church. I carried crutches with me, but really did not use them, taking them only because Mother insisted.

My leg, of course, remained shorter than the other, but there really was no more trouble with it.

I do not know why I should be so sensitive about it, but I am.

My mother is still living and is ready to testify to the validity of this miracle, and so would likewise all those who were present then in the church, if they still are alive.

—Mrs. Alice Kruger (Alexandra Chichineva)
Seattle, Washington
September 16, 1961

4. CHASTISEMENT FOR DRUNKENNESS
1903

VASSILY Skvortsov relates that on Spruce Island there lived a Hieromonk Nikita from Valaam, a missionary from Kenai Peninsula who had come to build a monastery there. He had a strong, stout constitution, and was in his prime. But he had a great weakness: he drank terribly! Once he was on his way to the village of Ouzinkie when he happened to meet an old monk who told him, threateningly, that if he didn't correct his way of life, he would perish. He told people about this himself at a time when there was no monk whatsoever on the island besides himself. Apparently he did not change his life, for at a later date the inhabitants of Spruce village, seeing the sky red, came there and found only the ashes of his hut, in which Fr. Nikita himself had burned. This was exactly at Christmas.*

Something else about Starets Herman and Spruce Island. This year ninety years have passed from the day of his blessed passing away in 1837.** It is a great pity that there is no one there. There were two families who settled there, but they started to make beer and carouse. The Starets quickly drove them away. Three children of one man died in a single week, and the other man died himself. Now the Starets again abides there in solitude.

—Archimandrite Gerasim Schmaltz
1927

* See Rev. Tikhon Shalamov, *Along the Missions* (in Russian) (New York, 1904).
** Actually, in 1836 (see the note on p. 36 above).

5. HEALING OF AN INJURED SHOULDER

VASSILY Skvortsov fell into an open hatch on a fishing boat in Kodiak and severely injured his shoulder on the cement bottom. He suffered from the pain for several days after returning to his home in the village of Ouzinkie. At that time there was no doctor in Kodiak and people were treated with home remedies. The more religious people, however, turned in prayer to God, to the Mother of God, and to the saints. And so it was that Vassily Skvortsov got in a boat and set out for the grave of Starets Herman.

In those days one couldn't get under the church (to the grave of the Starets), and everything was closed; only on the eastern side of the chapel some holes had been cut, and there people could reach inside and take some earth. That is what Vassily did, too: he thrust his hand into the opening, grabbed some earth and, baring his shoulder and hand and saying, "Well, good old man, I've come to you, help me," he rubbed the injured place with earth from the grave of Fr. Herman. And—the pain immediately disappeared and he returned home well. (Being an expert carpenter, he erected then and there, in remembrance of this event, a candlestand for the church in gratitude to Fr. Herman, and bore witness by this to the miracle of his healing.)

—Archimandrite Gerasim Schmaltz

6. HEALING OF MIGRAINE HEADACHES
1962

A CREOLE woman, Alexandra Kharalampievna Wotch, maiden name Ilarionova, suffered from shortage of breath and headaches. This old woman related the following to me:

"Mother used to tell us how, when Fr. Herman came to Kodiak, everyone would hurry to meet him and everywhere you would hear 'Apa has come, Apa has come,'" That was already during the last years of his life.

For many years she suffered from terrible headaches. When the government steamers came to Kodiak and there were doctors aboard, she would visit them. She took all kinds of medicine, but none of them ever did any good. And then finally she decided to make a pilgrimage to the grave of Fr. Herman. She got there without any trouble, without being bothered by shortage of breath (since the only way to get there is by sea, which is usually stormy). After praying at Fr. Herman's grave, she drank all she wanted from his spring, took some earth from his grave, and returned home to Kodiak, where she never again suffered from shortage of breath and headaches.

She died in Afognak and I gave her the last rites.

—Archimandrite Gerasim Schmaltz
October 31/November 13, 1962

7. FR. HERMAN'S PASCHAL VISITATION
1927 and 1935

A BOUT a hundred years ago the rumor reached Valaam Monastery, located on an island in Lake Ladoga, that one of the former residents of the monastery, the monk Herman, who left as a missionary to Alaska in the time of

Catherine the Great, was revered there as a saint. It was said that he had led a holy life and passed away in Alaska as a real saint. The abbot at Valaam then was the venerable Fr. Damascene. He quickly established contact with Alaska, and they started sending him information on the life and deeds of the blessed and humble monk Herman. With this information as a basis, a brief biography of him was soon compiled, and it, up to the present day, is the main source of information about this clairvoyant representative of Holy Russia and certain candidate for canonization as a saint of the Russian Orthodox Church.

Of extraordinary interest is one of his prophecies. It was fulfilled in our time, and in fact we are witnesses of it. Bishop Peter of New Archangel (Sitka), Vicar of the Kamchatka diocese, reported in his *Information on Fr. Herman* on May 21, 1867, the following prediction: "Still more he (Fr. Herman) used to say that although a long time would pass after his death, he would not be forgotten, and the place where he used to live would not be deserted; that a monk like himself, fleeing worldly glory, would come and live on Spruce Island."*

This prediction was fulfilled when the Very Rev. Archimandrite Gerasim Schmaltz came to live there. Fr. Gerasim left his native town of Alexin not far from Tula and entered the St. Tikhon of Kaluga Hermitage. This beautifully-located monastery was founded in the fifteenth century by a hermit, St. Tikhon, who at first lived there alone in the hollow of a great oak tree and dug a well, the waters of which became wonderworking. It flourished in the sixteenth century and became well known again late in the nineteenth century thanks to Optina Monastery, with which there was a constant contact.

* *Outline of the History of the American Orthodox Mission* (in Russian) (St. Petersburg: Valaam Monastery, 1894), p. 179.

It was there that Fr. Herman's disciple, Fr. Sergei Yanovsky, became a monk and died in 1876.

Fr. Gerasim left St. Tikhon's Monastery in 1915 and on
May 4th arrived in New York City. He came as a missionary
for the Russian Church and spent his first years in New York as
the bishop's helper, and then in Chicago, where he served as a
priest. In 1916 he came with Bishop Philip to Sitka, Alaska,
and in 1917 to Afognak Island north of Kodiak, where he
served as a priest for many years.

Fr. Gerasim visited Spruce Island for the first time in 1927,
and it was then that Fr. Herman called him. It was on May 27
(May 14 according to the Julian Calendar used by the
Church), soon after the Radiant Feast of Pascha. It was a quiet,
sunny morning. He was accompanied by Archpriest Nicholas
Kashevarov and two female pilgrims. It took them an hour and
a half to arrive by boat. On the site of the hut where Fr.
Herman had lived, and which had now completely disinte-
grated, there stood only a wooden memorial. A little farther on
there was a church over the grave of the blessed Starets, and
there Fr. Gerasim served a Pannikhida. It was a glorious day,
spring birds were singing, and Fr. Gerasim liked the spot very
much; it didn't seem like Alaska, but rather like some monastery in Russia. On the way back they again came to the clearing in the woods where Fr. Herman had lived and where on his
deathbed he had shone with the light of Mt. Tabor, his cell being filled with the fragrance of heavenly incense. While his
companions went on ahead, Fr. Gerasim got down on his
knees and, overwhelmed with joy, exclaimed: "Christ is risen,
Fr. Herman!" And suddenly he sensed in the air a marvelous
fragrance of incense surrounding him. He even shuddered. He
thought that it might have come from the cassock of Fr. Nicholas, but the latter was dressed in an overcoat and was already
too far away. And the aroma was such a fine one, and so

pleasant! With a quiet joy in his heart he then addressed the Starets as if he were alive: "I thank you, dear Starets, Fr. Herman, that you have found me worthy to visit this beloved spot of yours! Fr. Herman, I too have fallen dearly in love with this spot; if there should come a time when I will be able to come here to you to stay—accept me!" And Fr. Herman fulfilled his wish. Within nine years he had moved into the hermitage for good. But before that he had yet to suffer much.

When it became known that Fr. Gerasim was preparing to go to the island to live, the local clergy opposed this and resolved to prevent it. Vassily Skvortsov, who had intended to accompany Fr. Gerasim, came to him in Afognak and informed him that they were going to expel them from the hermitage with the aid of the police. He himself, out of fear, had decided not to go. Fr. Gerasim was very much affected by this, but he replied that if it wasn't going to be pleasing to Fr. Herman, then that's how it was going to be. He was so disturbed about it that before going to bed he hadn't even strength enough to say his prayers.

And then he had a dream, in which he was walking somewhere through a beautiful forest: spruce trees, in the distance a hill, and straight ahead a clearing with tall grass. And he heard someone pealing a bell and its sound joyfully echoing somewhere nearby. In the clearing he saw two bushy little spruce trees, and between them a monk of small stature with a thin little beard and wearing a small monk's cap. He smiled and greeted Fr. Gerasim, saying: "It is I who am here ringing the Paschal bells." And then kindly: "Batiushka,* don't be sad! It is Fr. S—y who stirs people against you. Have patience and all will pass!" At this the dream ended. In the morning Fr. Gerasim got up joyfully and resolved that there was no one to fear if Fr. Herman was with him. Following the advice of

---

* *Batiushka:* an endearing term for a priest or a monk.

Blessed Herman, he safely moved to Spruce Island on September 8, 1935. And he has been living there ever since, alone on the almost uninhabited island among the age-old spruce trees and gloomy storms.

No one besides Fr. Gerasim has lived so long on the island's holy site at Monk's Lagoon since the death of Blessed Herman. This gives us grounds to consider Fr. Gerasim as the very monk, "fleeing worldly glory," about whom the Wonder-worker of Alaska prophesied more than a hundred years ago.

During my pilgrimage to Fr. Herman's grave, Fr. Gerasim himself dictated all this information to me, on the twenty-seventh day of August in the year of our Lord 1961.

—Br. Gleb Podmoshensky
Boston, Massachusetts, 1962

8. HELP IN CHILDBIRTH

EMELIAN Petelin relates how a certain woman who had lived in the village of Ouzinkie always had difficulty in childbirth. She had had three children, and none of them had lived. She was again with child, and she had come to the island (to Monk's Lagoon on Spruce Island), believing that she would obtain help through the prayers of Fr. Herman.

She came to the spring, and with a prayer to Fr. Herman she drank from it all the water she wanted. She went back to the village by foot (it was about nine miles from the hermitage to Ouzinkie), on the narrow footpath which was all the swampy and almost impassable island afforded; and on the very night she returned to Ouzinkie, she gave birth. She was successfully delivered, and without any particular difficulty, of a child who survived to maturity.

—Archimandrite Gerasim Schmaltz
October 31/November 13, 1962

9. MIRACULOUS PRESERVATION OF FR. HERMAN'S THINGS
1943

I N the evening of June 17, 1943, there occurred a terrible fire that completely burned the historical church, together with its valuable treasures, in the city of Kodiak, Alaska. Here is how Archpriest Dimitry A. Khotovitsky describes it:

"Let whoever wishes say that this was chance, a coincidence; but here was a Divine Miracle. And our entire Alaskan and American Church should know about it.

"In the church of Kodiak, in the right annex, there were several articles: the monastic klobuk [hat], the cross, and the chains of Starets Herman. All of these were in a simple glass chest. And then the fire occurred, and everything got burned. The candlesticks melted from the fire, the bells melted, the walls were burned, but this klobuk was not touched, being barely scorched by the fire. The chains also quite escaped the fire, even though they were partly bound with leather—everything was left.

"When the psalm-reader brought everything to me wrapped in paper, and when my matushka* and I had looked at them—truly, I was so struck that I still cannot forget it. I crossed myself and kissed these things, and gave the psalm-reader strict instructions to keep them and give them to no one, and better still to take them to the grave of Starets Herman: these were his things, and they had been left undamaged through his prayers. Fr. Sinesy King said this: 'See, Father, how it was all fulfilled! Blessed Herman said that when the time came that people would begin to forget both the Church and their Faith, a Miracle would occur and a man of prayer would appear at his grave. See how it was fulfilled!'"

* *Matushka:* an endearing term for a priest's wife or a nun.

10. A RESCUE FROM PERSECUTION
IN THE SOVIET UNION
1936

B Y the prayers of Blessed Herman I obtained God's mercy in the year 1936.

I was banished from Kiev and lived under the surveillance of the G.P.U. in the district of Chernigov.

Horrible times began, known as *Ezhovshchina* (this was a period of wide and uncontrolled terrorism named after N. Ezhov, whom Stalin appointed as the head of N.K.V.D., when fifteen to twenty million people suffered in forced labor camps and many died). There were terrible reprisals. At that time I was reading *Ascetics of the Eighteenth and Nineteenth Centuries* (this was a collection of the Lives of saints who have not yet been canonized, issued not long before the Revolution in many volumes); as a matter of fact I was just reading about Blessed Herman.

Just at that time it was necessary to go and be registered, and I knew that at the time of registration many difficulties might arise for me in my situation, being a priest. And then there suddenly appeared a man who, absolutely unexpectedly, helped me to escape the possible reprisals. For me it was clear that this occurred through the intercession of the great Starets Herman.

And I wasn't just preserved there, but now too in America I live under the protection of his, Blessed Herman's, prayers.

—Archpriest Adrian Rymarenko
New Diveyevo Convent, New York

11. HEALING OF A CATARACT OF THE EYE
1947

On March 16, 1952, two inhabitants of the village of Afognak (located on the island of the same name, thirty miles by sea from Kodiak), Sergei Shirotin, fifty-six, and his wife Maria, fifty-three, related the following to me:

In 1947 their daughter Zina was attending school near Sitka. At the beginning of the year her eyes became diseased; she had to discontinue all her activities, and she was confined to the hospital. Towards summer she became better, but since the doctors categorically forbade her to read, she was confined to the house. On her arrival here the disease again broke out in her eyes. At first a small spot appeared on her right eye, but it began quickly to grow and cause pain. They went to a doctor in Kodiak, who determined that the cataract was malignant and that the patient was threatened with loss of sight in the right eye. The medicine given by the doctor did not ease the pain at all, and the patient spent practically her whole time in a half-darkened room. The girl fell into despair and thought herself doomed….

Zinaida's parents, Sergei and Maria, remembered the testament of their own parents: to appeal in misfortune to the help of Blessed Herman; and so, on the feast of the Dormition of the Most Holy Mother of God they set out to do reverence to the Blessed one and, following the custom of all pilgrims, they brought back with them water from the spring of Fr. Herman. "If you believe," said Maria to her daughter, "Fr. Herman will help you." With these words she dipped a handkerchief in the water that had been brought back, and applied it to the eyes of the sick girl. The first touch of the handkerchief caused great pain, but after that the pain at once ceased; and after a month of washing the eyes with the water from the spring, the cataract disappeared completely and sight was restored. Since last year Zinaida Shirotina has been wearing glasses, but over the eye that was once diseased there is plain glass; a special lens was necessary only for the other eye.

Since everyone who participated in these events lives here and is in good health, I appealed to the doctor for an explanation, and he told me, word for word, the following: "You know, Father, that miracles occur in this world: I've been convinced of this more than once in my practice as a surgeon. So in the case of Zinaida Shirotina it was a clear miracle." The testimony of the doctor evoked in me a feeling of devout reverence for Blessed Herman, and I decided to communicate this to all Orthodox people, so that they might render thanks for us to the Lord our benefactor.

—Archpriest Alexander Popov
Kodiak, Alaska, 1952

12. HEALING OF PARALYSIS
1936

THE earth from Fr. Herman's grave is considered to have healing properties. Here is what one resident of Karluk village related to me last summer.

In 1936 a married couple, Peter and Yuliana Naumov, then living in Chief Point on the western part of Kodiak Island, had a fourth child born to them. The Naumov family lived absolutely alone in Chief Point and looked after the nearby lighthouse. There was no doctor, no obstetric nurse, not even a midwife present at the birth, and the husband happened to be out repairing the lighthouses.

She was in long and difficult labor, and as a result her

whole right side was paralyzed from head to foot; she had been in perfect health up to that time.

The husband returned and, seeing the pathetic condition of his wife and four small children, fell into despair. There was no telephone or telegraph there; a mail ship came there just once a month bringing the necessities of life; and it was only when driven ashore by bad weather that a rare fishing boat put in. A doctor was necessary, but where would one go with an absolutely motionless wife and four little children in the harsh Alaskan wintertime? One couldn't leave the wife and children alone for a long time either, since the trip to the nearest settlement would take more than twenty-four hours. Peter was torn between the children and the sick wife, not knowing what to do or where to begin. Gradually, however, he gained control of himself and started trying all kinds of home remedies; but alas, they did not do any good, and only increased the poor woman's misery. The husband finally came to the point where he was going to put his wife and children in a boat and take them to a doctor in Kodiak, but the sick woman protested. They finally decided to try the last remedy that was once used by the Alutiiqs: to rub the paralyzed part of the body in order to cause an increased circulation of blood; but the sick woman, it turned out, did not react at all to the stimulus—the paralysis was complete. Peter sought every sort of help in vain, and finally he turned to God.

While praying he remembered the story of the Alutiiq Egor Kaliglyou (who died fifteen years ago)—how paralysis had struck him and deprived him of the use of his left arm, but how with mud consisting of earth from the grave of Blessed Herman mixed with holy water Egor had rubbed his afflicted arm and been healed.

When he had finished praying, Peter—enlightened—turned to his wife and ecstatically cried out: "Herman,

Herman!" His wife by signs indicated the icon-case, where some earth from the grave of Blessed Herman was kept. Peter stirred the earth into some holy water and offered his wife as much as she could drink (it should be said here that for two days she had not been able to swallow at all). "I had to make an effort to pour the drink into her mouth, and I don't know whether she drank any or not," said Peter. Right after this he stirred in some more earth, explained again to his wife what this was, and began to rub her paralyzed body. "How long I rubbed, or which prayers I said, I do not remember ... but Father, you see Yulia yourself—and that is my whole story. Others may think what they like, but from that time on in our icon-case we have had, together with the other icons, a portrait of Blessed Herman...."

Silence followed, as each of us prayed mentally to Blessed Herman.... Before me sat a healthy woman of thirty-eight, in the prime of life. I looked attentively at her and then at the image of Blessed Herman—his black monastic cloak, his bent hands holding his prayer-rope, and I forgot that I had come to have dinner with Peter; I had come to behold the Divine world....

I remember this story now while standing at the grave of Blessed Herman, and I bend down and take some earth for myself....

On the way back I once again stopped in at the church, and then at the chapel. My companions have left the chapel-cell of Blessed Herman (on the site of which, in a little log cabin, Fr. Herman met his righteous death) to reinvigorate their physical powers, but I once more begin to contemplate and to kiss the relics of Blessed Herman.

—Archpriest Alexander Popov
Kodiak, Alaska, May, 1951

13. HEALING FROM CANCER
1951

I WOULD like to tell about one case of miraculous help from Blessed Herman. It occurred in our own time, and I can personally attest to its authenticity. A certain man had been sick for three months from some kind of malignant tumor on the foot. This greatly impeded his walking, and the pain was so great that he was unable to stand it without some sort of pain-relieving ointment.

He never had the opportunity to go to a doctor, since at first he spent a long time in Displaced Persons' camps, and then he moved from Europe to America. Thus there was no possibility for him to receive thorough treatment.

At length there was long-awaited America and a peaceful life in Springfield, Vermont. He used the first money he earned to go to a doctor. That was in the month of May. The doctor treated him for three weeks and then said, word for word, the following: "Please forgive me, but I do not understand what is wrong with your foot. You should go to the hospital."

In the hospital they took X rays. The doctors consulted and said that they would have to wait for the arrival of a specialist who was supposed to come soon from a nearby city, Hanover, Vermont.

"Fear and anguish took possession of me," related this man. "I knew that I could not avoid an operation.

"Since I would probably have to be sent to a neighboring large city for the operation, it would require more money than someone newly arrived would have, and there was no one to borrow from. The situation was very serious. But there was nothing that could be done about it; I had to consent, since the doctors were very alarmed about the symptoms of the disease."

On the evening before the day on which he had to go to the X-ray specialist who had come, and from whom was expected an authoritative opinion on the cause of the illness, the sick man turned with warm prayer to the help of Blessed Herman, the wonderworker of Alaska, with whose life he had previously become acquainted.

In the morning they went to the hospital. The physician carefully examined the affected place, went out to those who had accompanied the sick man, and said, "I seriously fear that it is cancer. It cannot be operated on. We will try the only remedy left, but of course without any guarantee. Only do not speak about it to the patient, so as not to frighten him...."

The doctor returned to the patient and told him that instead of an operation they would treat him with X-rays.

Giving thanks to Blessed Herman that an expensive operation was not required, the patient gladly consented to the Roentgen treatment, not even suspecting what terrible danger was hanging over him.

And then the miracle occurred. Under the action of the Roentgen treatment—in the course of altogether nine minutes—the pain disappeared and did not begin again, even though there was swelling for two weeks more. Within a month and a half there remained not a single sign of this terrible disease from which he had suffered constantly for three months. And only then did the doctor say that the patient should thank God for being healed of cancer.

Marvelous is God in His Saints, the God of Israel.

—Archpriest Stephan Lyashevsky, 1951

EDITORS' NOTE: The above incident occurred to the author himself, but for some reason he chose to describe it in the third person.

14. THE SAINT'S LESSON THROUGH HIS SPRING

I N the city of Kodiak up to the present time there has lived a certain V. K., a Protestant by faith, who is married to one of the granddaughters of the ever-memorable Archpriest Nicholas Kashevarov, a very zealous daughter of the Holy Orthodox Church. Mr. V. K. likes to have a drink; however, he never gets seriously drunk. By nature he likes fishing and hunting. Every year, whether the fishing was good or bad, he would unfailingly go to Spruce Island to go visiting, as he said, with Blessed Herman and Archimandrite Gerasim, who was living at that time on the island and was the guardian of the relics and objects relating to Fr. Herman. Unfailingly V. K. would visit the chapel built on the site of Fr. Herman's cell and would admire and marvel at the Elder's chains that were kept there, his preserved kamilavka [hat] and other objects connected with the Elder's life. He would ascend to the church, in which the Saint's remains were found, and, although not Orthodox, would bow down before the Saint's tomb with the Saint's image covering it, and place a candle. Then he would go to visit Fr. Gerasim, and before leaving he would go to the spring to drink the cold, pure water, take this water home at his wife's instruction, and set out on the return trip.

This time V. K. was not alone, but with other residents of Kodiak. On the way to the spring V. K. remembered his wife's request to bring St. Herman's water. But he had no bottle, except for a bottle with wine which was being saved for the return trip. Without thinking long about it V. K. drank the contents, proposing to rinse the bottle and fill it with Fr. Herman's water.

Coming to the spring, however, V. K. saw that the water was as if boiling, raising to the surface various kinds of filth, and for as long as V. K. waited the water continued to be turbulent, becoming muddy and unsuitable for drinking. And so he left for Kodiak, without drinking the water or bringing any home.

"For a long time," V. K. told me, "I told no one of this, but I didn't stop thinking of what had happened until I went again to Spruce Island." This time he took with him no "provisions." After landing on Spruce Island, he went immediately to the spring. The water was transparent, as pure as tears! "I drank the water for a long time and came to believe that the Elder, showing me such a sign, was really a man of holy life," he told me. Having returned home, he related what had happened to him. And from that time no one would dare to go to Spruce Island again without proper reverence, but would go there to venerate the Saint and be refreshed by his holy water.

This incident, so similar to the incident of St. Seraphim of Sarov and the Decembrist at the spring—whose suddenly muddy waters, the Saint related, were a sign of the evil nature of this revolutionary's schemes—has never appeared in print before. Wondrous is God in His saints!

—Archpriest Alexander Popov

15. A MIRACULOUS HEALING THROUGH EARTH FROM THE SAINT'S GRAVE

ON this very day, August 16 by the new calendar, in the house of Alexander and Maria Baumann, there were guests; and their daughter, twelve-year-old Elizabeth (Liza), became sick just at the most inopportune time. By five in the afternoon pains appeared in her stomach, and they increased with every hour. The poor mother was torn between the guests and her sick daughter. No medicines did any good. Finally, at eight in the evening, Liza said in tears that she had no more strength to endure it—and generally she is a patient child. At such an hour on Sunday it is difficult to find a doctor, and, besides, there were guests....

The mother remembered that she had earth from the grave of St. Herman, sent to her by a friend, and because of the canonization this earth was lying on a table nearby. She prayed fervently to St. Herman and said to her Liza: "Pray hard to St. Herman and put the envelope with earth on the sore place." The girl had barely managed to place the envelope with earth on the sore place and turn over on her side, when in an instant she fell sound asleep! To be sure, around 2:30 in the morning the pains returned and again began to increase. The father wasn't home, and without him they didn't want to do anything. While they waited for him the girl again became unable to endure the pain, and the mother in despair again hastened for help to St. Herman. This time she poured two or three pinches of earth into holy water, following the example of Naumova, and praying fervently gave it to Liza to drink. In about ten minutes the pain completely passed and the girl became well.

The next day they called a doctor all the same, more in order to find out what kind of pains these had been. He diagnosed an attack of appendicitis, but reassured them that the appendix was now in such a condition that there was no danger and one could forget about it.

—M. Hoerschelmann, 1970

St. Herman prophesying to Constantine, an Alutiiq boy: "My child, remember that on this place there will be a monastery in time." (From the original Life of St. Herman, written in 1864 at Valaam Monastery.)

PART III

SPRUCE ISLAND

Pilgrimage to Spruce Island

S TEPPING onto the shore of Monk's Lagoon, one immediately senses a deep peace underlying the physical beauty of the surroundings. Since St. Herman's time, little has changed at the site of his struggles—no roads, no phones, and no electricity. The unsullied beauty of the island presents a reflection of Paradise: towering cliffs, the dense Spruce forest with its moss-covered floor, soaring eagles, salmon jumping in the calm waters, and fox and deer roaming the beach.

Every year, natives, pilgrims and travelers from around the world come to visit the home of America's first Saint—Fr. Herman, the wonderworker of Alaska. Here, Fr. Herman lived in prayer and fasting, cultivating the earth and fishing the local salmon to feed his native orphans. Those who come collect earth from the Saint's gravesite and water from his miraculous spring. Many healings have been recorded over the years and continue to occur. Others come simply to pray and seek direction in their lives.

At the north end of the beach, a footpath leads into the woods. As the surrounding trees silence the hum of wave and wind, the visiting pilgrim is welcomed by icons of Orthodox saints housed on the trunks of aged spruce trees. The rattle of daily cares and thoughts vanishes before the silence of the emerald forest.

Several hundred steps up the path, one comes upon the

hermitage of Archimandrite Gerasim Schmaltz (†1969). Before St. Herman's repose in 1836, he prophesied "that a monk like himself, fleeing worldly glory, would come to live on Spruce Island." When Archimandrite Gerasim came to stay for good at Monk's Lagoon in 1935, this prophesy was fulfilled. As a young monk he had been formed in the spiritually thriving atmosphere of pre-revolutionary Russia, and grew up in contact with the renowned Elders of Optina Monastery. After five years at the St. Tikhon of Kaluga Monastery, the young monk left Russia to seek the monastic ideal on the holy mountain of Athos.* Here, Fr. Gerasim came into contact with holy men and was introduced to the hermitic life, which he would later emulate in Alaska.

In 1912, Fr. Gerasim returned home to Russia. At this point his life took an unexpected change as he was sent to America as a missionary. Arriving in New York in 1915, he was ordained to the priesthood and sent to Alaska, where he was assigned as the village priest of Afognak (near Kodiak). Due to the Bolshevik Revolution, he would never return to his beloved homeland. At this newly assigned post, he served faithfully for nineteen years until he received a mystical calling from St. Herman to move to Monks' Lagoon. For the next thirty-five years Fr. Gerasim prayerfully kept watch over the relics of St. Herman and persevered amidst the stormy Alaskan wilds. He also became the beloved pastor of the nearby village of Ouzinkie.

Today his Russian-style log cell stands as it did during his lifetime. Beside his cell is a small chapel, which he built on the site where St. Herman once lived. Dedicated to the Kaluga Icon of the Mother of God, the chapel preserves the memory of Fr. Gerasim through his personal icons which still grace the

---

* A peninsula on the Aegean Sea in Greece entirely dedicated to monastic life. Over the last one thousand years, Mount Athos has been a center of Orthodox spirituality and asceticism.

walls. In recent years, both the cell and the chapel have been renewed. Here also lies the grave of Fr. Gerasim.

Buried next to Fr. Gerasim is the exceptional married priest, Fr. Peter Kreta, who served the city of Kodiak and the neighboring villages. Fr. Peter dearly loved Monk's Lagoon and as a young man he would offer his time for the upkeep of the holy sites. When he passed away in 1995 it was his final wish to be buried at Monk's Lagoon.

Forty steps from Fr. Gerasim's hermitage, surrounded by ferns and moss, lies the miracle-working spring of St. Herman. Year round, crystal clear water flows from the very spring that once refreshed the Saint. It is the pious duty of each pilgrim to drink lavishly from this spring and take some of the holy water home as a blessing from St. Herman.

Returning again to the main footpath and walking a few more paces, one reaches the final destination of this blessed path: the grave of St. Herman. In 1898 a church was erected over the Saint's resting place. This simple rustic structure, made of hand-hewn logs and wood shingles, is dedicated to the founders of St. Herman's Valaam Monastery, Sts. Sergius and Herman.

In 1935 the chapel was restored under the direction of Fr. Gerasim, at which time St. Herman's relics were uncovered and placed in a reliquary inside the church. Here, alone in the woods before the holy relics of the Saint, Fr. Gerasim poured out his prayers before God for three decades. And though the earthly remains of St. Herman were transferred to Kodiak at his canonization in 1970, the presence of America's patron Saint remains on the spot where his soul was translated into eternal life.

—Ryassaphore-monk Andrew
St. Michael's Skete
Spruce Island, Alaska

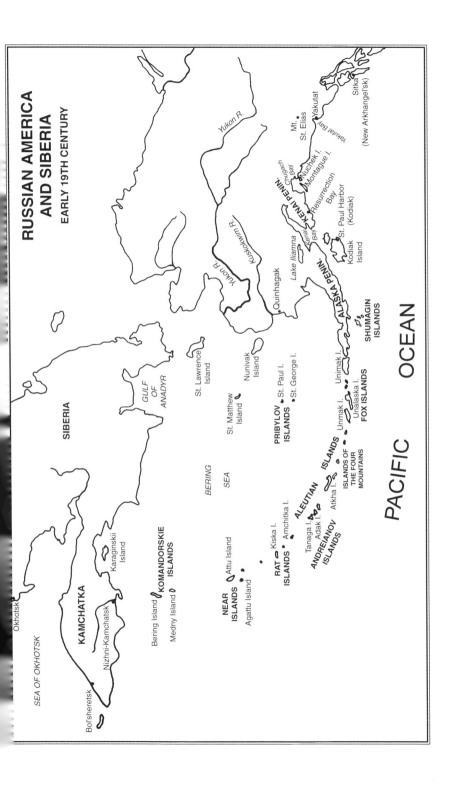

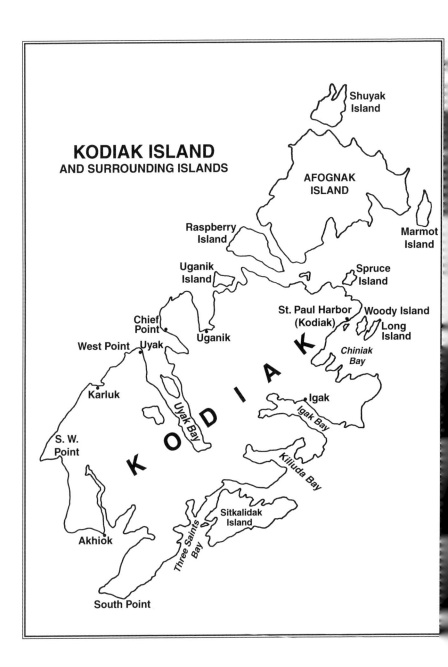

KODIAK ISLAND
AND SURROUNDING ISLANDS

Shuyak Island

AFOGNAK ISLAND

Marmot Island

Raspberry Island

Uganik Island

Spruce Island

St. Paul Harbor (Kodiak)

Woody Island

Long Island

Chief Point

Uganik

Chiniak Bay

West Point

Uyak

K O D I A K

Uyak Bay

Karluk

Igak

Igak Bay

S. W. Point

Kiliuda Bay

Sitkalidak Island

Akhiok

Three Saints Bay

South Point

ABOUT THE ARTIST

Nikki McClure lives in Olympia, Washington with her husband Jay T. Scott. She cuts her pictures from paper using an artist's knife. Her work has been shown in the United States, Canada, Sweden and Japan, and has adorned books, wall calendars and greeting cards. She has spent two Junes on Spruce Island, Alaska, walking in the mossy forest where St. Herman lived.

ST. HERMAN OF ALASKA BROTHERHOOD

Since 1965, the St. Herman Brotherhood has been publishing
works of Orthodox Christian spirituality.
Write for our free 88-page catalogue, featuring over sixty titles
of published and forthcoming books and magazines.

St. Herman of Alaska Brotherhood
P. O. Box 70, Platina, CA 96076

You can also view our catalogue online, and order online, at
sainthermanpress.com